At Once

At Once

❧ Poems by

Jenny Browne

[signature: Jenny Browne]

🯅 UNIVERSITY OF TAMPA PRESS • TAMPA, FLORIDA • 2003

Copyright © 2003 by Jenny Browne
Cover painting copyright © 2003 by Stella Alesi
All rights reserved

ISBN 1-879852-87-X (pbk)

The cover painting is "Untitled (Daisy)" by Stella Alesi. Oil on wood. 30 x 30 inches. 2001.

Designed and typeset in Libretto types by Richard Mathews

Manufactured in the United States of America
Printed on acid-free paper ∞

University of Tampa Press
401 West Kennedy Blvd.
Tampa, FL 33606

Browse & order online at

http://utpress.ut.edu

Library of Congress Cataloging in Publication Data

Browne, Jenny.

At Once: poems / by Jenny Browne.
  p. cm.

  ISBN 1-879852-87-X (pbk. : alk. paper)
  I. Title.
PS3602.R735 A95 2003
811'.6--dc21

                         2003005225

Contents

I.

For the Morning ❖ 1
In Case of Disaster Break Me ❖ 2
On P and 1/2 Street ❖ 4
San Antonio ❖ 6
Three Blocks Between ❖ 7
Evidence ❖ 9
There Will Be a Sign ❖ 11
Sky Burial ❖ 12
Bigger Compared To ❖ 14
What a Heart Does Best ❖ 16
A Year Ago This ❖ 18

II.

After a God ❖ 23
Anticipation ❖ 24
Saying Yes ❖ 25
This Love ❖ 27
Rainsong ❖ 29
Married ❖ 31
Testing the Waters ❖ 33
Heart-shaped ❖ 35
In the Low Country ❖ 37
Open ❖ 38

Here ❖ 39
Blood ❖ 40
The Medicine Disconnects Her Mind from Her Brain ❖ 42
The Announcement of My Birth ❖ 43
Advice ❖ 44

III.

At the Yak Hotel ❖ 47
Up Again ❖ 48
In the Dark ❖ 50
You Can Make the Whole Journey That Way ❖ 52
(Have This) ❖ 53
Nourish ❖ 55
To Fish in Shallow Water ❖ 56
"A Hand That Bears a Thick-Leaved Fruit" ❖ 58
Grand ❖ 59
Twin Cities, No Sign ❖ 61
Starry ❖ 63
Before ❖ 64
Native Grasses ❖ 65
In the Garden for the Blind ❖ 67
Field Trip ❖ 68
Down from Provence ❖ 70
Recognizable ❖ 73
30th Birthday Poem ❖ 74

IV.

On Massage ❖ 79
Little Proof ❖ 80
If God Agrees ❖ 81
Love with the Africans ❖ 83
Shelf Life ❖ 85
In Boquillas Everything ❖ 87
Never Mind Over Matter ❖ 89
Essay on Idleness ❖ 91
Show and Tell ❖ 93
The One That Got Away ❖ 95
Valentine ❖ 97
Last Call ❖ 99
Out of Context ❖ 100
2001 ❖ 101
The Middle of America ❖ 103

Acknowledgments ❖ 107
Notes ❖ 108
About the Artist ❖ 110
About the Author ❖ 111
About the Book ❖ 112

> *I reason, Earth is short—*
> *And Anguish—absolute—*
> *And many hurt,*
> *But, what of that?*
>
>   –Emily Dickinson

> *... I'll tell you—I understand*
> *How come the dancing bear tore off his skirt*
> *And headed back to the Yukon,*
> *How come all of a sudden jewels in avalanche*
> *Down the spine of my sleep ...*
>
>   –Thomas Lux

I.

For the Morning

spiral of glory
poised on the vine
I never tire

of your white trumpet blazing,
flared edge
of color all

open to the oceanic
sort of end, thrashing red
snapper on the line,

an entire face falling
at the glacier's
distant crack.

Flower turning back
to the used-up
tissue, sticky

as the stillbirth?
Just as much work.
You don't know how much

you can really give.
You don't know how to live
but at once.

In Case of Disaster Break Me

On the island the sea is not the sea.
It is a water braid
always coming undone but coming
is the wrong verb for the waiting.

On the island waiting is a place
back of the brain that drags
out buckets and knows best the pitch
of water close to overflow.

On the island the evacuation route
is the busiest street.
You pass blue signs
picking up the kids, pumping gas.

They seem to shudder in the idle
or maybe I am shuddering
because I don't believe
in natural disasters, only human ones.

A woman at the next table groans
and says *yes, this is a small town
but I wouldn't want to paint it.*
And would you cling to anything

like a wall with the whole mind
surrounded? How do you live
with that kind of peeling pain?
But see I meant to write peeling paint

but that's no disaster. It means
on the island I believe in chance,
the Styrofoam cup hurled blind
to the churning cricket.

I believe
because I don't live
on the island.

On P and 1/2 Street

Lips explain a face
while passing air
just begs for a whistle.

A prayer wobbles
on the corner. *Now what
       I done done, Lord?
Where I go go?*

What the dark arc of doorway overhears
I don't know, know exactly.

Every leaf of her body shivers.

This listening in motion is something
like the way the interpreter reads
my poem with his hands
and decides

clenching means pleasure and perfume
means smell and maybe it does.

The way *drive by* fits inside
a sentence like *we took a Sunday
drive by the sea*. Something dark
inside something wide. Something
like shouting *fire!* and hoping
the sky can sign.

Signals from each skinny
smoking piece of ground.
All the kids I'm driving home say
this is where I stay
and never where I live.

San Antonio

I learned to walk in this town
which means I learned to fall.

Criss-cross of the temporary
hopscotch blocks.

Rain come, chalk message go.

Something else never there
reappears. Childhood
a stranger's name
rising from every brick
in the backyard. I stack them

until sound is brick repeated,
until everything
sticks together and overlaps.

The abandoned head of a piñata
still dares a sudden breeze.

One photograph is taken
at an angle so we're holding
up the moon.

That was my thumb.
This is my mouthful.

Three Blocks Between

You do not know me
until you know this. A little marker,
little end, broken tail raised
again in the circling wind.

You do not know there are only three
blocks between McKinley Elementary
and the corner brick house
with her million needles

stuck in the trees. That doesn't seem
room to walk the full power
of the human
into an eight-year-old brain.

Eight about the perfect year
between days you could spend
just swinging your arms
if only because they were arms

and yours and could be swung
and the two-numbered years so much
heavier in the hands. Never enough
fingers sticky as gloves

of hairspray and sand.
Eight the year you realize you can
put a bead of wheat between your teeth
and it might let you in.

You too can become
a small thing with a big story.
How the power of the human
is to mean to. Not kill maybe

but scare the squirrel frozen
in fear like they get   then sent
scurrying before the steel
-belted wheels.

You can walk three blocks alone
and love only
the skip clip of your own
heels leaping to stomp.

Evidence

Because the body remembers when I paid
my little sister dimes by the minute
to scratch letters down the pale inside
of my forearm during church. Relief
is a rising red road width of a fingernail
on the map somewhere between
a little pain and distraction *This-is*
-boring. I-am-hungry,
our Methodist game of hangman
from the pew where nobody died
only dangled.

Later her unlocked book left turning
pages like the motion of time
passing in old movies
or the flip books making the shape
of a child running
        out of lines *listen*
-to-me.

Little One, is there anything else?
An ash I could spread over
your first body
like some comic book detective
taking fingerprints left places

you didn't even know how to spell?

We could burn the letters

and use the black remembering
to write a different story. Here,
have the soft part

of another arm, two hands, my eyes
that should have been watching.

There Will Be a Sign

When the warden removes his glasses
it means the needle can open up
her fat mouth and sing.

The chaplain likes to put his hand
there just below the inmate's knee.
He says *my job is to hold up
a mirror of our world.*

One time a boy asked *Father
what do I say? What
do I say when
I see God?*

They say the sound
of a man's breath
leaving
is like a released balloon
sputtering damp.

They say there is no sound
like the one a mother makes.

At the end one began to sing
"Silent Night."
        *Round young virgin
mother and*

child was as far as he got.

Sky Burial

You can not see the circle
of stained stones from the path.
Arch back and you may
watch a different curve,
        vulture orbit without end
or beginning circles
the sky's laundry line
of flapping faded prayers.

Vultures are the hint
of a body taken higher.
Wind, carry the hint
of voice from stone, voice of tin
        bells in the courtyard wailing
above a plastic-wrapped mound
gathering flies, circling dogs.

In the puddle by the temple door
a reflection of movement, truest proof
of our fugitive selves, body
in a ripple disappearing. *And so what
do you know about losing?*
Only everything
I know.

Come morning I know
two monks will unwrap the plastic
and flop the curled brown body
onto the faded scarlet stones.

They will chop her into sections;
      piece she loved with by
piece that listened, heavy human
piece that keeps you
from turning from this. Bones
pulled clean, crushed
to dust. Bone to dust,

      a rhythm, this life
to feed another. There is this
life to feed another.

Bigger Compared To

If I could remember Cadillac Mountain I would
inhale the first sunrise and my only year
as the only. I'd hush

the new brother coming in months
to make me bigger compared to
which is all bigger really means.

I would remember the radiating heat of a lobster
held above the foamy pot
and watch the air swallow itself

wet along the pier. The dark pattern
of Dad's wool honeymoon sweater left
marks on my cheek pressed to his back

those early years in Maine when he examined
the lungs of potato farmers' sons. Could they inhale
the yellow gas and keep going?

If I could have talked I would have whispered,
don't move a muscle, in the left ear of each
pale shaky boy and hoped for no motion

from the kneecap thumped with a rubber triangle
just weeks before it would explode in one Vietnamese
slow-clicking step.

This long before my father's own brother swelled
and swallowed a death multiplied inside, before
the smaller sister fell out of the sky.

This is 1973, twenty-five years before another night
when he wakes sweating and sprinting towards a child
slipping from the coast's black boulder teeth.

Which is why he remembers some steps
I never took better than ones I did. And this
the year he will wish to live backwards

one-false-step-doctor's-frown-permanent-airplane-ticket
at a time as each day boils him
a little deeper.

I don't think he meant to grow so tender,
meat forking easily from inside
the cracked shell

which must be why he looks somehow sadder
after a vacation back to Bar Harbor where he stood
on the pier night after cold clear night pointing

at the lobster tank like some sunburned god
half wishing they all didn't look so alive before
nodding *yes, that's the one I want.*

What a Heart Does Best

Beneath tubes of trembling
yellow light a teacher warns
against lust and gluttony, the only two
deadly sins with any style.

She doesn't use those exact words
but they know what she means
and I want to know where her high road leads
besides out of view of the glimmer

in this valley where a six-year-old boy says
when my heart hurts it feels like someone
punched me in the permanent teeth.
He says permanent

as in deadly, lasting or intending to last
like we intended those days to last
when the worst we knew
we would lose was teeth.

So lady you can leave me here,
knees bent and pressed against the cold
green linoleum of the past wishing
I again had fewer years than sins,

wishing all I knew about a heart is what
that boy's class does when I ask
what theirs do. The whole room breaks
into a flapping, fingers folded as in church

and steeple. They thump the butts
of their palms like the pounding of two
bodies convincing two hearts all they have
lost is worth this coming together

and those children turn their faces up
insisting what a heart does best is somehow
keep itself beating *like this, Miss.*
Mine goes like this.

A Year Ago This

The weaver fingers her wool and says *think
a year ago this was grass,* handful of seed,
beating hearts between her fingers.

I think dreadlocks
on these old craft fair hippies and how
I've always wanted to feel

the heavy release of one sawed
loose into my palm.
Not all would fall

with the first cut but I wonder
if much ever does? A year ago
one answer to that question

would be the whole of a life, every strand
torn from the sky but this is not another
poem about plane crashes coming down.

Only a January morning
and the small voice of steamed milk
here to keep something warm.

A year ago that was grass too.
A year ago there was no grass
over Jane's grave, only a square of earth

recently lifted and replaced
like the bald arc along the edge of the yard
where we laid a live wire

then buckled two sparks
against the white dog's throat.
He ran beeping circles for weeks

but by the end of the year realized
if you move fast enough
it might only hurt for a second.

II.

After a God

The man I love most says one day
he will take a ballpoint pen and connect
the stars across this freckled
scoop of chest and milky way.
We'll cross the slope
of pale belly and name
the new constellation after a god
who shows people
all the places they might shine.

Anticipation

Glittering snip of tinsel
makes like a fire.

From here it was all *baby baby baby*!
A blood-thumping
muscle going crumble.

Green Light
and nobody moves.

Pink and white blooms both
vote for the same
floppy branch of oleander.

Did the book say poison? Don't ask
me or the wasp moving
towards that something

sweet drifting out your mouth.

Saying Yes

Somehow my voice sounds sure
as sugar concentrating her story
into all a wine grape knows, one drop
between perfect and ruin.

Anything worth doing
is that close to losing.
But this zoom on one
life close-up feels easy
as following the eye
of a single fish in the confetti spread
of the whole school's rippling fins.
Feels easy but you are so close
to each wrong one.
They say it's impossible
to really tell the difference.

Still my gills glitter
in all the new places we are breathing.
Everywhere I look is looking up
through water. Don't ask from which drop
this joy echoes. I only know words
to the song your breath makes
blowing across the tops of bottles.
Music made in the space
between any old fullness and you.

Later when a child asks me
to give her some hard words
to look up in the dictionary

I can't think of one.

I tell her I like sentences
that end in then.

This Love

suggests unfinished stone, scratched surface cracks
where roots decided to listen in, spread palms

sprouting vines, a changing color visible
from the road. This house suggests

slow surrender, pears ripening in the window
behind the essence of white curtains, brushing

of winter hands, gloveless gathering
scattered papers from the wind. His fingers

suggest sanctuary or the curve of a lean
bone tea cup, protection

of twiggy toad backs, light bulb thin
saffron threads, heat passing

through reinforced concrete, a hidden
welded strength. This life

suggests crossing a Denali creek,
and the throbbing after fast

frigid gulps, bare toes numb knocking
into sharp rocks, one rushing sound

then blood staining water, warming to feeling
This poem suggests a woman listening

for desire in the muffled lives rising
behind a hallway of thin numbered doors.

She makes left turns until she finds
a quiet where she left it, propped open

by a book of blank pages and gentle
man still sleeping. This poem suggests choosing.

Rainsong

> *Let the rain kiss you.*
> *Let the rain beat upon your head . . .*
> —Langston Hughes

So easy to worship anything,
drizzle in a second language,
that reflected gratitude shining
back from one fat drop
considering her possibilities.

How I hate to pass an open hand
over the balanced kisses
on a wool sweater sleeve,
layer of light collapsing. Look
I have nothing against soaking it in.

How we'd pile out of the fake
wood-paneled Buick mid-sentence,
day or vacation to my father
with his arms flung skyward
in an imperative to absorb. *Come on, kids*

extract this moment from the rest.
And we'd try to guide it out
like the heart or funny bone
from that Operation game stashed
in the backseat and wince

at the angry buzz, always surprising
though we knew it would happen

eventually like this rain in the middle
of August, drought days before our wedding,
wedding the act, like the wedding

of one drop fast piggy-backing the next,
all the charm of momentum.
There is no precedent for this soaking
contentment. We are rolling love.
Even my freckles making

like rabbits, litters of light left
from a more obvious day.
One so near
the insistence of collar bone
sings that you missed her.

Married

Leaving San Antonio I crumble
another cloudless handful
of sky, sharp as luck
at the edge of tonight, the first night
I believe the coming stars

require no wish. They blur
into the passed over
red walls of women, once red
skin peeling free, the red-tipped
needles on a cactus cheek, any old hook
of regret releasing, any voice but ours
dark between shining.

In my lap, the unzipped bag of advice
says remember you asked for it.
I say remember *why*.

Not for the fleeting ping
these new rings would make
from a fist
knocked on the lasting
mountain's cracked chin. Don't test it
or stop to hear a red-headed vulture
ruffle on a dead mesquite.

In the morning sit together
on a sun-stained ledge and bloom
your hands open

with bread for those two
fat blue jays, two
handfuls of the new
sky and they will come
and eat. They will eat.

Testing the Waters

Drug test pap smear oil change all
in the short of a single day.
Fluids in a row like ducks of course
only I don't even get high
since the time freshman year
feeding the ducks on Lake Mendota
when the mallard crowd turned
on the female, surrounded her, clamped
the lean neck and pushed until
she drowned white belly up before
our six-stunned bloodshot eyes.

I was thirty before I tried again,
before I stopped hating nature altogether,
the clotted five days of it, low back
and lower art, a different paranoia
in swollen extremities like I'd become
a blue-tongued giraffe licking salt slow-
blink through my high metal bars.

All this before I finally stood still at all
let alone with a man who vowed
not only to change
all my filters but to daily
kiss the same place low
on the neck the ducks know
most vulnerable. Exactly where
to grab and force a face down
or up but when I looked

at him that day he only whispered,
can you see yourself

in my eyes? And I promised
I'd make him coffee and hold on
to my keys and try
to complete my sentences and then
we lived . . .

Heart-shaped

The two-headed vase
with a black-backed crack
up the middle means
it was baked, means
we are married.

So does the beep-ba-beep
of the heart-shaped
waffle iron, cabinet door
snap to the rattle
of 33 new glass bowls
that fit inside each other
like smug Russian dolls.

Stuffed under the sink,
the lavender plastic sack,
claimed kit of the necessary
"for the newly married"
from the city office
where you can also take on
an assumed name.

Take the cool handle
to any one of our steaming
nonstick surfaces.
It means you can touch them
anytime and you can
touch me now.
We've got tongs,

hand-tooled Appalachian spoons,
a juicer, jelly-roll, the fold-out
vinyl camping couch for two!

Settling into it for the first time
our hip corners knock, barely
bruise that joint where I best bend
and may last break. Feel
how it hurts how
it holds.

In the Low Country

Whose blood is that,
smacked from mosquito
to the flat of my thigh?

How they call you?
Cobbled breath of river night,
mossy cascading back

of Savannah morning
ever mourning. The end
of night. How so early

in what was now dead
Uncle Carl's high bed
you moved inside

the space water makes
moving through
the low country

to an ever-widening ocean,
the whole holy-rolling
Intercoastal Waterway turning

sand to island. Bearing up
the extended she-crab claw
and cupped oyster

shell upon shell as if
they could surface on their own
that wide, surprised and shiny.

Open

The tremble this time of year,

Six ceiling fan blades never catch up
with the idea they spin of themselves,

a whirring background
to the splat of perfect
gutter love for the single
inch of red iron rail.

Sweat shadow making green
sheets black in the shape
of a snow angel. Limbs flailed
with that flurried abandon.
Could they have ever
been mine?

Ping of the metal mind.
Broken glass broken glass
how fine you sounded how
thirsty I am

Never trust a man
who says
it's *only* water.

Here

Where twenty-five
minutes of Mingus costs
a quarter, grease

and forgiveness

can be expected.
Nothing dies

slow as the smell
of fried
onions (thank
God) and when

eating like this

is in style again
I will bet
my stomach against
the way a mind
keeps trying.
I have never been

this full.

Baby, let's go make us
some kids just
to bring them
here.

Blood

They play red gypsy songs
and bring a whirling

birthday dance, two little girls
in purple shoes. All sparkle

and stomp on the stripped-
down wood. Soles smacking

shake the caliche walls.
They were born in this house.

I began to be born this day
below the Ferris wheel, 1971

Wisconsin State Fair, breaking
water, spreading blurry

circles of light. Tonight
the phone call from an old friend

with a newborn voice saying
The truest thing is your body

already knows how.
So far my body only knows

how to dance
with these children,

with the thought. Imagine
putting on a coat

of ocean, all the waves asking
are you ready yet?

Are you ever ready?

Remember the flat cactus
paddies left by the porch,

a thought to plant later
taking root, blooming blood

red fruit, the only color
a body knows for sure.

The Medicine Disconnects Her Mind from Her Brain

The doctor meant *her mouth*. Oh the sharp chiseled chin
of the mistake jutting in accidental profile.

After one of my own I'd like to say wrong name, wrong birth.
That wasn't my brain or mouth asking when she is due,
such singular rushing blood beneath the broad belly.

My midwife friend retells the one
about the beaming Nordic pair, perfect
circle of blond blue-eyed genes, nodding father
and the shiny black hair, fine Asian eyes
wailing between his wife's strong thighs.

You would think if there was even a chance
she would have prepared him,
said, *the cherries are falling,* Japanese for
are you sitting down?

So here's to all the ways of wrapping bad news
in a clean cotton towel and toting it next door.
Could be muffins. Could be a joke. Could be Toto
and the useless click of Dorothy's backpedaling.

Oh to rent the smug expressions
on our future children's faces,
the way they will look flat at every undeniable lie
disconnecting the mistake from the mind, from time.
Did you ever? No I never.

The Announcement of My Birth

is tri-folded with four slits
and a window for the face.

It looks so much older
than my life.

Not as stunning
as I don't remember it.

Mom's script with a shaky
loop in the y. Black eyes

that are blue. Both hands intact
and wrapped tight

as the recent past
dries high on my forehead.

Pink and blue lines on which to sign
in either case

Name of Father. Name of Mother.
How casual when they remember

that they were the first
ones to ever have a baby.

Advice

My father warned
> *when in doubt*

downshift.

Mom said *leave things*
better than you find them
especially bathrooms
        and hearts.

Grandmother Browne's tips for marriage
became the stuff of legend, a whisper
on her only daughter's wedding night.
Remember every age together
is the best age. Be hot in bed
and get yourself an egg pan.

Of course she denied it
until the very end
just like she denied being
nearly two years older
than grandfather all sixty-one
they were married.

He said *never write anything down*
that you wouldn't want
the whole world to read.

III.

At the Yak Hotel

The clerk always smiles
(or squints) in such
constant Buddhist sunshine.
Spit hits the high air here
already drying
and I begin
a new sentence before
finishing this one
and clean up
lunch before we stop
chewing and ready
by mid-afternoon for
tomorrow ask her
*when does the sun come up
in Lhasa?* She smiles
(or squints) and says
in the morning.

Up Again

before most this time stripe
and cruelty somehow stripped
of his bright blue hard hat.

So let's make this an ode
to the soft tissues.

If you're a being, hurt's a been
and who's responsible
for holding on to the dead?
For once it seems
you can leave that
to the hanging bellies
of vultures shifting in the balcony
of someone else's dumpster.

This new waking life has a better
flight to decay ratio. Think a kite
made from every page
of the Clean Air Act.
Oh say can you look
faith in the open mouth
like a perch gasping, like
a breeze catching
the top hat,
        oh the lift
on that thing. *Abracadabra*

being one of the only English words
with absolutely no meaning. Nothing
stays put like yesterday.
I am not making light of this.
Sometimes I still have trouble
spelling tomorrow.

In the Dark

Learning from pain should be quick
not like this charred
life of a wooden spoon
caught again by cast iron.
Ash on all sides
reminds my hands.

Even after the smoke signals
I take longer
than the flight of September arriving
to the blind South Texas summer,
      delay weeks blinking
on the arrival board while hijacked
roadside daisies wilt in your arms.

We need so many more chances
      an entire bloody night
wrenching porcupine quills
from a dog's tongue
for the second time this spring.
You have to push deeper
before they come free.
I never get it

just right, the technique
for a cynic's one-eyed take
Still have to blink first, hustle up
a little backbone behind the flimsy
blond lashes and pause

before one tries again
to open slow and forgetting
all it learned along the damp
dark road home.

You Can Make the Whole Journey That Way

Under the moonlit soapsud
clouds scrubbing at darkness.
FIRE DANGER EXTREME
screams from the shoulder
with the radio silent
seeking circles beyond
its own remembered places.

We're farther west than we've been
when you cut the headlights, melt glass
between us and night and ask
how's the air
in or out there where voice
becomes the white line
guiding a silence.

Only the crackling grass below
one wind's evaporating
remembers all the work
of living, sun to vein.
A green verse fading
to brown to underfoot
for only this

full minute stop
all the reaching
up and out and lean
      back a little. Lose some
warning time and feel wise.

(Have This)

Ground wears the going sun well today.
Your shoes fit.
All the music escaping
car windows sounds like soul.

Let your heart if it can dance
a little wider. Dance
to the echoing ding of sometime,
passing tap of the now.

Be an instant
immigrant to the shores
of remembered kindness.

One old sign points
to the element of surprise
but the path from satisfying to magic
is not well marked.

You are on it
when a jogger passes
and hands over a perfect
sand dollar, the first
your hands have held.
His voice paddles
a calm below the coast's
shoving breath, *If it breaks
let the angels out.*

They may not be angels,
ones who leave us like that,
light and lasting.

But they have wings
like distant birds, black
parentheses on sky hovering
above an entire day
        saying only here,
I want you to have this.

Nourish

And there was the wind of oranges
lifting from fingertips

And there is a peeling of words
at some tables, tedious
as taking the skin
from each grape to taste
its shadow. To define what
the light on wine
is really trying to say.

Soon the night
and there is a woman I love
who says I always wonder
what I am supposed to be
catching up to

I love her
because she says things like that
and uses words like nourish.

Serves them one at a time
upon an open palm
where they can believe
in the taste of their own skin
like you can believe in yours
when the whole ocean
is watching.

To Fish in Shallow Water

You might imitate a Calusa chief
and order the cracked shells
of two hundred years too much
crab-eating piled into a mound
shape of a donut, deep in the middle
of the Everglades.

Then you could watch
the daily green returning
fill the sunken eye and creep back
leaving only silver
gasping within reach.

Then if the calcium deposit of memory
is all that remains of Calusa
you might bum a ride
with three sunburnt men, 24 Bud Lights
and two dozen bait shrimp twitching
in a fat plastic cup.

When the spine of the boat knifes
the sucking low tide bottom
know nothing
but enough waiting will float you
back to motion.

And you can still say you've been fishing.

But if you fly down to the fragile
index finger of Florida and never
paddle through the southern
mangrove-blocked veins where
barnacle-shod roots walk on water
and the gumbo-limbo peel
their red paper dreams of disappearing

you might have to settle
for watching a waiter from New York
flick his gold-chained wrist and fling
chunks of untouched sourdough
through the bayside window
until the fish come and knock
on those bobbing black-water
reflections of moon.

"A Hand That Bears a Thick-Leaved Fruit"

The first taste of the Everglades
is not the speckled yellow gator-egg
bubble gum in miniature cartons
stacked at the tourist shop counter.

It is older. It could be
something dying, something swallowing.
Anything deep-fried
and half-baked that leaves crumbs
stuck in the seams
of your backteeth.

Deep Florida's breath is heavy
as the first boy's tongue
stretched there to fill
your mouth with its thick
spongy pink. I can still taste it
one mile out, one foot down.
One in, one up, the predictable
pace of the Gulf Coast.

I try to remember
when kissing was what you did
and did.
Before there was somewhere else to go.
Before you got in the boat
and heard the ranger remind, *You fall out
you canoe you just stand up.*

The closest land is the bottom.

Grand

> *Since there is no nature,*
> *since there is not human nature, I suppose we can be done with it,*
>
> *the whole business of matching trees with moral lessons,*
> *the past set against the future.*
>   – Ira Sadoff

This National Park Service brochure does not list
which ribbons of sky and canyon officially
look best stretched together.
Two Germans argue for the stunned
maroon and black-blue just past sunset. It is best
right now I am thinking. Any right now.
But how close is too close to thinking at all.
That the mind could even wrap its little rank
around an absence this full. Just try
to take the Grand Canyon personally.

Try to write your way around the edge
of meaning with her bottom kicked clean out.
And still farther out on the rim-road
tumbleweeds careen into car grills.
Hand with iron splinters hand with twig.
Which hand has the glue?
Did you really think you could
put it all back together with your two
blue eyes, five going-numb fingers? Go ahead.
Arrive after dark knowing
it is out there. Go find the canyon with
the beam of my tiny metal light. Don't forget

to trace the grand whole
of remembering we barely exist, another lift
of chest, a pine needle falling still
falling.

Twin Cities, No Sign

Before every well-insulated house
a car breathes with no body.

I follow the three-pronged
pace of the winged, head

for the circling gray, one
of a thousand lakes, days, walks.

My boots are heavier than usual,
heavier than boots.

Even the slush hushing
too much, too much

of this human filling up
and in, opposite of tree

branches skinny and scratched
black against sky. Blurry line

between lake and lifetime.
But don't send the search party

out for my voice. I know it
takes two full inches of ice

to hold a body. I'm just edgy,
following the hidden bank, following

the ink-dipped goose ends,
surfacing buoys of belief

in the beneath. Half a being
broken by another

snowflake's circle changing
the surface without a sound.

Starry

Think how the murmur
blue vase of rose-bellied
lilies can fill a space.
Could make a tunnel
from look to stay, green
to breathe. Might even
help explain the sensual
rub of conjunction
to that skidding relief
you get on a path
beyond the screened-in
yard next door. Not porch
but yard but what do I know
of outside but this
pedestrian panorama
from a purple tent pitched
a mile from the trailhead,
instant black beans swelling
in a red recycled mug.

Think how Van Gogh painted
all of nature one color
until someone finally saw it
his way. Until someone mentions
a starry night and we think
of him, think of the yellow swirling
search for your place, blurry
learning to praise it.

Before

the yellow pine floor was *done*

then mopped, carpets flopped,
warped windows

shaking as the spin cycle begins

there was another place
and footprints
        before boards Wind
before breathing Leaves
glittering in the back-light.

Out front a telephone pole leans
into lost voices.

They painted this porch ceiling
to look like sky
but now the pale
blue is peeling free.

The bees were never fooled.

Someone missed the corners
Left Cloud Left Cloud

Native Grasses

Strange to dig this shallow
and expect anything
to grow. What we scatter
is said to have roots
that know the way.

To slide a spade
in at this flat angle, nearly flush
with a plan to welcome
the from-here-low-
maintenance-grow-to-
thigh-high varieties.

Not to dig really but to lift
the surface, untangle
bottom knots of always green.
We do it for the promise
in the picture, for the sound
of their sparking names, Little Bluestem,
Sandoat Grama. For the predictable
line of shovel pressing a steady
refrain through the waffled
rubber sole.

We do it for an excuse
to loosen the work talk that rises
like water to the red palm, tender bubbles,
silent filling like sunrise to stinging

release   until you   me   the dirt
the hands   all stand
skinned and blinking
in one small spot that remembers.

In the Garden for the Blind

You can tell the name of one leaf by the fuzzy
raised roads along the backside
but this spreading red flash beneath
the grasshopper's wing means
you're too close.

We're close enough
to the source of this steamy spring to notice
which places it takes her slick sulfur offering
longest to dry, crescent crack
just below each breast. On the thighs
dull gray coins of shade, color of forget,
black box of childhood beeping
back to life, black stripes
smeared under our eyes

like we had fly balls to catch
like we didn't know better
than to look right at the sun.

Field Trip

Three rows of wood ears pressed
to the chest of the dead cedar
while grimy vines still listen for breathing,
the silence of everything
turning back to dirt.

A small hand opens, offering
the dusky owl pellet, embedded
rat claws in gray fluff then points
to a blue ice cube tray sunk
by the Bayou half full

of muddy water, full
of muddy sky.
I ask them to write
what they can't see, roots
of the Resurrection Fern clutching

up too high, the constant dying
of their own cell-splitting
bone skin minds.
*But don't put that
Spanish Moss in your backpack*

We can't see the new lives
waiting inside. I can't see
what might have been
any different day deep
as the Congo of a child's asking.

Dark of heartness what
behind the blue? A full sky
behind the smallest eye?
What for the red water
winking back like a sign?

Down from Provence

Crack of a chip-chipping ax tip
down against stone
rebounds from the sternum
where the two nearest hills
come together. There's a valley
carved between, low swallow
surrendering to the level
out and back we pick clean.

It brings blood to the stomach
like that pink fire distilled
from stem and seed, leftover
like the blue-black stain
of grapes darkening
the palm's winding predictions
of a love so much longer
than any life.

In the next row the juggler's hands
are also stained. He grips
a cigarette between his lips,
tosses the knives high
and sings in Spanish
tu no tienes la culpa mi amour,
There is no blame
on the path between vines,

just limp leaves, thick clay
and stones all the bending

cleaves to our backs
so when we reach
low for a flat one
to skip on the beach at Nice
we remember.
I remember all the stones

had a pale stripe
across their bellies, the seam
where gray meets light,
surprises itself or falls apart
wondering which way to turn.
You know there are as many ways
to be bright as to grow dark.
Fill your pockets with them.

Balance time on flat surfaces,
windowsills, backs and days
when all you carry is a bucket
and wind beating a come-on
drum for hours, the same
slow moment rotating lean
weeks around the iron sun dial.
We owe it

all a quiet quaking awe, all
the green upturned leaves, morning's
newest silver gathering
to let go and all those

scalped cork trees lining
a falling-away road down
from Provence. It takes nine years
for their bark to fatten

enough to be useful, trunks
stripped clean leaving moist
auburn marrow. Thousands
of perfect circles punched
through the thickness, perfect size
to squeeze inside this aching
stone hand, to hold in
still so much
aging before I'm ready.

Recognizable

I've been rumored to cut the blue
from bread and stare far
too long.

To make more than the occasional
Uppercase Mistake

and dig on through the backyard
garden full of red holes
        width of lost
seedlings all the while
knowing the blood-root of bamboo
is coming back.

Pulling it makes a fire
of my palms
        from the friction,
the question. Where is root? Stem?
Still asking the mud-caked
mud-cracked hand.

Now remind me again how I know you.

30th Birthday Poem

Isn't this one of those Self-Guided Tours
like the one where Roger Moore's 007 voice
fills the hire-a-headphones kit you get
in Beijing's Forbidden City?
The one that gets you
all the way to the grown-ups' table
cutting your own meat and grieving
the loop-di-loop green souvenir straw
you once slurped dry?

My mother used to make me sing
the words to Happy Birthday
as I washed my hands. The verses
just enough time to kill germs.
And I say I know the way
but I still spend years in some towns
following the first route I learned
even though they say *direct* is a word
I could try. Even though the big red dot
on the shopping mall wall affirms only
YOU ARE STILL HERE.

But there is this new ring
in the stump of me like the ring
in the stump of you. Most variation
in the time it takes people to notice
you're watching them, have been watching
thirty-some done and still wondering
who really knows

if the tumbling geometry of the far-off
flock lifting and opening
has a detail map or back-up plan.
Birds never seem to notice
you're staring again.

And I still don't know
who I'd ask
to be the voice for the tour
of my Forbidden City.
I know about open doors
from spiders' dreams and the knocking
about these knees making
long pale stretches
in the best jeans. Only fading
another way to be grateful.

IV.

On Massage

The mouth attached
to the hands gripping
the feet says this
is deep tissue.

And the tissue says
no kidding.

Then the hands
find the spot
bone center
of the heel
where we impact
the earth.

And the spot
wonders if it always
has to hurt.

Little Proof

of movement on this compacted
stretch of sand. No shape
of walk or stand. Only the splatter,
nameless birds scurrying
after the surf and back,
a round-trip on the string
tied to our breathing.

It could be a good shelling day
but every fluted edge
and polished curl I bend towards
has something still alive inside,
the weight it takes
to make a mark on this earth.

We come upon a lone frenzied
patch all scratch-blur
of hands and dug-in
heels that could be left
from the late loving or later fight
or someone's turned-over
life shaken down
and poked a little with a stick.

How we ooze and slump
back into the smooth walls
of our long-shaped escapes.
I mean who knows
what all humans will do
when they're feeling small?

If God Agrees

> ... *most of the time, 'chopping,' as they call it,*
> *wasn't meant to convey or accomplish anything* ...
> -James Traub

My husband says I'm the only woman he knows
to go after cockroaches with a bread knife
and get them.

Must have been five pieces,
weary antennae still twitching
from the trash this morning.

Back in Freetown I used to watch them,
a crackling dance from my cot flat
in a cement box lit by kerosene, two by two

the jerking cockroach waltz. On that hall
all the walls had light switches
that hadn't worked in thirty years.

I flicked mine every night
because that was its name. It had nothing to do
with expecting light.

But I came to expect the nightly drill, to sleep
dreaming the way things can grow
so much larger from a distance, magnified

by a choking flame. Wings and bent legs
becoming flags and trees, becoming dreams
I am having about cockroaches

and the chopped-off hands of Sierra Leone,
machete nights slashing open the sky, puddles
of blood balling in the dust.

Fifty thousand hands waving back
from the dirt road ditches and what-were
windows of burned out Bo Town.

I joke about the collective shudder I have just sent
through the broader cockroach community and forget
this is how it works in some places, the official plan

to turn the person into the thing you go after swinging
a stone-sharpened knife, aiming for parts that once made them
most human, thumbs, earlobes and shame.

In a photo I cut from the newspaper, a man
with one hand and no lips holds a cigarette
to the mouth of another.

His name was Abraham.
His name was Brima.
They never expected the chopping.

When I lived in Freetown we would dance
to a twisted reggae version of *Another Day
In Paradise*. My friends would clap their hands

and turn the lifelines up to the sky, faithful
prayer to any *why*. A sign
that means *if God agrees*.

Love with the Africans

The Americans compare notes.
*Did he pinch your nipple hard
as you would grip the head
of a crooked nail and tug?*

*Did he say I love you and want
to possess you the first day
you passed a scrambled taxi corner
squeezing the singing mouth
of a thin-skinned orange
to your peeling pink lips?*

Did you know that meant *let's
have a Star Beer and let
the bottle sweat rain down our knees? Let's
peel the labels off and press them into damp
tattoos on our piano key thighs*, mine
wide and white, nicked with freckles.
His two tightropes of night.

My knees could still weep
for the name, *Panga,* word for knife,
and I believed the blood metal taste of it
would not leave my tongue
like a scar, black spot through a fingernail, proof
of the hammer's pounding heart, black
going purple moving up month by more distant month
until there was nothing to show for
the flash then throbbing taking skin

from any thing and twisting it
into a red-faced promise that means
so much more than it means because I am nineteen
and looking for anything the color of change.

I am looking for anything to bring home
besides a cheap shoepolish-stained statue
from the market and parasites
with all their swollen names. I don't tell
the other Americans that I smooth
drops of my own sweat along his railroad
of scars rising like polished regret.
They will never be mine.
I don't admit that for a moment
I think I know something, anything, about love
with the Africans.

Shelf Life

West Africans offer half the sky
and their last bite of rice,
equally valuable but I refuse
Bintu's sticky sandwiches. The jar of mayonnaise
she opened last month waits
smudged and silent on the only shelf
in this sweaty dormitory
on a Freetown mountain ledge
sharpening a year of Star Beer
smoky sunsets and something
like salmonella.

Every sunrise her cracked brown hands
with two smooth pink faces grip
the gummy jar, twist the rusted lid
and spread a thick blanket on three cents
worth of soft white bread. I cling
like the mayo to an old story
about potato salad and summer picnics
and when she doesn't up and die
on the next cot my cultural rule of thumb
is slammed in a foreign car door.

On out the window fly the others
       —swimming in lightning, smoking
at the pump, the whole pasteurized lot.
Here there are no expiration dates,
no blurry purple numbers predicting
the moment a belief passes its prime.

I know there is a difference
between carving out the blue spot
and discarding the whole turkey
to make some room but the fridge door
in this mind is closed, a stubborn little light
still shining on that vacuum-sealed
world of single servings
and a shelf life longer than the human guaranteed
to always taste the same.

In Boquillas Everything

costs a dollar, the delicate scorpion
bent and woven from copper wire.

It's the fee for crossing
the famished Rio Grande

in a red boat called *La Enchilada*.
For purple crystals spread on card tables

in the front yard of a blind girl
picking her teeth with a fat cactus spine.

Spots of blood dry just below her lower lip.
Wan dolla her brother yelps

flapping two dozen neon bracelets
strung across a slap of cardboard.

Then *something for me yes?* He means
another dollar and you have them

in your pocket, folded into fourths
and warm. A dollar can even buy you

a picture with Juan Crazy but he
may try for $5 and wave with that arm

healed at a stomach-turning wide angle.
He's gotten more demanding

since someone put him up
on a white gallery wall.

But you will wrap your fingers
around the deep brown silence

of his shoulder and wait
for the flash. You will wrap

your fingers around the bone
smooth freedom of a stick, abandoned.

And you will keep looking
for something no one wants

and feel rich as the fuzzy
air left in your pockets.

Never Mind over Matter

> *You cannot do nothing.*
> –Simone Weil

All doubt begins with something small
        say the weightless
head of a bird almost floating
on the full spring grass. I cannot feel

my rubber toe turn it
over by the brown hooked beak. It is perfect
without wings to be broken, claws to dig
into anything alive.

Hold it high, the almost pinch
of nothingness peeked at through a black
bubble of disbelief
that used to be an eye.

Find a bird like this and you can almost believe
they are right.
It is cleaner, somehow closer to God
not to want a body, not to be

so attached. I try to quiet
the jerked clomp a clomp of the mind,
hush any hotshot
thoughts dropped from on high

still wearing their heavy-heeled
firefighter boots. From the burning belly

watch the breath thicken until it fits
through a hole the size of a wing,

shape of a heart breaking, some wonder
twin reflection of wants. Never mind
any air we breathe these days
is fleeced with worry, blurry in the heat.

Never mind the sweating sweet
orange stench of judgement like trash
is fast to burn, slower
to disappear. I could sit here and be

smoke trying not to vote fire
but my doubt begins the moment
I can hold a head in my hands
and feel nothing.

Essay on Idleness

> *You should never put the new antlers of a deer*
> *to your nose and smell them. They have little insects that*
> *crawl into the nose and devour the brain.*
> —Kenko

What of the hidden danger
in drawing an infinity symbol
in the pollen puddle forming
on your desk.

Report on the sunflower's surrender:
It's the weight of the bloom
that ruins everything.

It's the weight of the head
that isn't holding
its own here.

The telephone psychic asks if I have a scar
on my knee,
        slender crescent curving
below the chin? Am I hard on myself?
Have I ever lost
one earring? A dozen keys
that could open? This brain
devoured in the attempt
to eat pretzels all the way around
without breaking through.

Fingernails ripped with the grain.
No peace in the tiny
yellow cranes folded
from square Post-it notes.

Shoes on, shoes off.
Watch on, watch off.
Enough of this

rain and the walls are left standing
with nails rusted to red
dust in their own narrow holes. Like pollen
or sand. On some beaches
the sun goes down
and everybody claps.

Show and Tell

> *Like a guy in a bra,*
> *it's the idea that counts.*
> —Greg Brown

Except I keep picturing the guy,
sharp nervy sweat, hairy barrel-
chested bind, and not the why.

And when the stereo is stolen from the car,
red and white wires stretched naked
from their dashboard cave, I like the idea
that *Transcendental Blues* is still inside
but it doesn't really count for much.

Still if you say you'll be back at 10
it doesn't really matter if it's 12 or 2
I'm pissed and you get the idea.
And if the Yankees lose 15 or 3
to 2, they still lose
not just the idea but the game.

My friend Dom is still trying
to get used to the idea
of his lesbian pagan real estate agent.
What greater cosmic glass
does playing hardball smash?
But it's on past the 90s
and didn't someone just remind me
that this decade the image is dead?
What matters is the concept

that a car once missed the turn
in front of my high school
and mowed down the cloud
at Cancer Corner where the hoodlums
smoked between classes. Not how
the metal bench curled up like burning paper,
not the jean jacket, white high-tops,
pale cheek of a boy smeared
across that cold idyllic street.

The One That Got Away

Milky tea whispering one
curled fern of steam, new
pencil sharpening into a perfect
swirl so delicate I can not bear.
Even when I think I'm ready,
there it sits, shivering strand
of web between what
we wanted and what
we're given teasing
the lone bulb's try at self-illumination.
Now you see me

       silver sign of snail, angle
of knowing anything
for sure. *And now you don't*
but when did the game begin?
I'm still out back squatting
under the mulberry tree, counting
backwards from twenty
thinking you won't see me,
hands pressed this hard
over open eyes.

This is not the game
where anything freezes and stays
when you touch it. In this one
it is a vase of white petals
letting go because air knows
you are getting warmer.

There is no water left, no green
wire wrapped round the stem.
This is just a song
        for the ones who got away,
prisoners of war propped up
on rusty knives saying what
they want to hear, while the eyes
blink *don't believe*
        a word. And for me,
listening too closely to see

cloud that was a rooster,
ripple to prove the stone.

Valentine

If I give you red paper and black pen
could you draw me a heart
equal size on both sides?

I will cut it out, double-side tape it
to the cracked wall and wait
until it fades, until I'm not sure
it's mine, the way you sometimes
don't recognize a word common
as *the* or tricky like *rhythm*
and have to repeat it until
you're sure that can't be right.

Maybe then I'd see
what gives first, swells or point,
how a heart fades and where
the colors go, land for the overflow
of recognizable things.

Like just today I have lost
the location of a street called Water,
words to a song about Saturday night
pimpled face to a hand
that touched my knee
beneath a table (not the name
of the pizza place, pepperoni
taste on his tongue).

I can't see Annie
who dressed like a bruise

that Halloween I was a cat.
Are there bruises from this,
      opposite of impact,
the thinning blood of available
space, watching your own
face in the glass so close
both word and mouth disappear?

Last Call

Behind me
a lady says *I knew it was bad*
when someone offered me $50 for my underwear
and I asked if they wanted new or used.

Why does her faded black
T-shirt look so much softer
than a white one would?

And why does it seem
somehow healthier
to roll your own cigarettes.

And buddy what do you mean
your mustache is older than I am?

Where oh where my mind goes
when I see a big big woman holding
a small small man?

The old Mexican takes off his hat, turns
and whispers, *Those pretty girls by the fire*
don't know it yet but they're gonna smell
like smoked hams come morning.

The guy from the flour mill asks,
How many pairs of shoes do you have?
My wife has 32,
      32 pairs of shoes . . .

He finishes his Lone Star
and stares at his hands.

Out of Context

Half inch of dust
on the barely moving fan blade.
Just how much hurt can stack
a thin face unnoticed.

They say there is always something
to be made of anger. But what
of the slower accumulation. Only this
still do I even see that anything repeated
even the even
spin of happiness is taken
out of context. Even happiness again
but how else would you want
to take the world

but in your grandfather's stiff canvas coat
with a five-year-old lottery ticket soft
in the breast pocket. We all need a place
to keep what gets us through, the sound say

of a gray cat chewing
from two rooms away.

2001

To think I once believed
the wide-open mouths of last year's
three zeros meant there was room
to turn all the way around.

And tonight the charged
changed air around the ancient
creaking gas heaters
has the gray cat padding in circles.

Twin strings of the dusty beige
window blinds are knotted
and hung with sleeping
new faces, blond families
dressed in denim, holiday bushes caught
in a net of blinking lights,
Santa on a Harley with big
biker love from Ray and RayKay.

Five of my fingers are trying
to pick out the Farewell Blues
on a mid-Missouri mandolin.
A loose limb changes the time, taps
on the frosted square of sight
still opaque in the corners
with fear or weariness, the same
thickness tonight and still
under the tree a brown paper-wrapped
package from the past.

I'm not going to open it.
Do you hear what I hear, the thumping
of its bubble-battened heart?

The Middle of America

Gripping both leather armrests
    the child thinks
she makes the train sway.

There are things you don't know
you can do until you are
doing them;
    hollandaise, oil changes,
back walkovers down the aisle
of the Southwest Chief.

From the observation car
you can watch the wind
behind a fence push a swing
50 feet across the lawn.

A dog wants to play catch
but won't let go.

When people on the plains look
at the sky they are waiting
for it to turn green, not frogs
    sure sign of hail,
all the classifications, nickel-sized
to softball. *You should see it*

here in the middle of America;

black socks and sandals.
A record store on Rt. 66

is called Mecca and it's Beef Empire Days
in Garden City,
        the municipal band doing *Spoonful of Sugar*
in the park
and I don't know what to wear
anywhere anymore.

A woman and all she owns

sits in a chair at the library, head tilted
as if reading not sleeping as if
this needed rain could change its mind
halfway down, catch itself.
But I saw it. But I didn't

want to stop here.

Acknowledgments

Many thanks to the following journals in which some of these poems first appeared:

Another Chicago Magazine: "The Medicine Disconnects Her Mind from Her Brain";
5AM: "Last Call";
Kalliope: "This Love";
Many Mountains Moving: "In the Dark";
Permafrost: "Here";
Post Road: "Twin Cities, No Sign" and "Before";
Rhino: "The Middle of America";
San Antonio Current: "What a Heart Does Best" (under the title "Like This");
Seneca Review: "Essay on Idleness"

Additional thanks to the Writers League of Texas and the Vermont Studio Center for generous funding and time, to the Browne, Rose, and Martin clans for love unconditional coupled with enough chaos to keep it interesting, to the Lousy Literary Band for laughter in the key of G, and always to Scott, my favorite reason for anything.

Notes

The lines from Emily Dickinson are the first stanza to poem #301.

The excerpt by Thomas Lux is from his poem "Farmers."

The title "A Hand That Bears a Thick-Leaved Fruit" is from Wallace Stevens' poem "O Florida, Venereal Soil."

The excerpt by Langston Hughes is from his poem "April Rain Song."

The excerpt by Ira Sadoff is from his poem "At the Grand Canyon."

The lines from Kenko are from his "Essays on Idleness #149."

The lines from Greg Brown are from his song "Slant 6 Mind" found on the album of the same title.

"In Case of Disaster, Break Me" owes much to Elizabeth Bishop's poem "One Art."

"Evidence" is for Bugger.

"Bigger Compared To" is for Tom Browne.

"(Have This)" is for Peter Davis.

"Nourish" is for Joal Donovan.

"Blood" is for Becca.

"On Massage" is for the hands and heart of Lesley Marcus.

The James Traub quotation is from "The Worst Place on Earth," an essay on Sierra Leone that appeared in *The New York Review of Books*, vol. 47, no. 11, June 29, 2000.

"Valentine" is for Anne Meckstroth.

"Field Trip" owes its life to the students of Trinity Episcopal School, Galveston, Texas.

About the Artist

Stella Alesi is a painter and photographer based in Austin, Texas. She received her MFA from the University of Massachusetts-Amherst in 1991. Her painting reproduced on the cover is one of a series she completed while in residence at the Vermont Studio Center in 2001.

About the Author

Jenny Browne has traveled, lived, and worked in West Africa, Central and South America, Asia, Eastern Europe, and Southern France. She has built toilets, picked grapes, kneaded dough, coached soccer, worked as a journalist, and taught English. Now she lives in a hundred-year-old house in San Antonio, Texas, where she works as a poet in the schools and directs the Literary Arts Program at the Good Samaritan Center. Her poems have been published in numerous journals, displayed on public buses in Austin, Texas, through the Poetry in Motion program, and included in two anthologies for teenagers, *What Have You Lost* (Greenwillow/Harper Collins, 2001) and *Is This Forever or What* (Greenwillow/Harper Collins, 2004). She was a 2002 Writers League of Texas Poetry Fellow and her chapbook *Glass* was published in 2000 by Pecan Grove Press.

About the Book

At Once is set in Libretto types designed by Swedish typographer Torbjörn Olsson. His original inspiration was the roman and italic lettering of Ludovico degli Arrighi, the 16th century Italian calligrapher whose work also inspired Centaur and Arrighi types. Using the roman letter forms he discovered in handwritten opera librettos, Olsson first designed a font he called Ludovico. Later, deciding that Ludovico was "too weak for smaller text," Olsson designed Libretto, "with a larger x-height, bolder, and more modern, but with some medieval feeling." The book was designed and typeset by Richard Mathews at the University of Tampa Press.